Awe- inspiring
Present

of Affirmation

Sharmaine Scott ~ Author

Copyright © 2020

by Copyright By Sharmaine Scott

ISBN: 9798612059615

Printed in United State of America

Inspiration Page:

This volume is dedicated to my children. Self-affirmations, increasing self-esteem and self-worth should be taught early, why not teach these important principles along with the ABC's?

A
Amazingly Awesome

You are Amazingly Awesome!

You are Admired for being

Authentic

B
Brilliantly Beautiful

You are Brilliantly Beautiful!

Beloved, you are Blessed and

Brave.

C

Charismatic and Confident

You are Charismatic and

Confident!

You are Celebrated for your

Compassion and Charity

D

Devoted and Disciplined

You are Discipline and

Devoted!

You are Divine, Delightful, and

Dependable.

E

Efficient and Electrifying

You are Efficient and Electrifying!

You are Exalted, Eloquent, an Empowering.

F

Fancy and Flawless

You are Fancy and Flawless!

You are First-Class, Fearless,

Fashionable and Fabulous

G

Genuinely Gracious

You are Genuinely Gracious!

You are Goal-Oriented, and

Good-Hearted.

H

Happily, Harmonize

You are Happily Harmonize!

You are Humble, Helpful, and Honest

I

Intellectually Intoxicating

You are Intellectually Intoxicating!

You are Important, Inspiring and Imaginative

J
Justice and Justified

You have a strong sense of

Justice and you are Justified

You are Joyous and free of

Judgement

K

Kind-Hearted

You are Kind-Hearted

You are Knowledgeable and

Kind

L

Loving and Loyalty

You are Loving and Loyal!

You have Longevity and

Lovable Leadership.

M

Mighty Majestic Master

You are a Mighty Majestic Master!

You are Miraculous, Magical, and Mighty.

N
Naturally Nourishing

You are Naturally

Nourishing!

You are Noteworthy,

Noticeable and Necessary

O

Optimistic and Observant

You are Optimistic and Observant!

You are outgoing, Original and Outstanding

P
Powerful

You are Powerful!

You are Passionate, Peaceful,

and Precious

Q
Qualified

You are Qualified!

You are Quick-Thinking, and

Quotable

R
Respectful

You are Respectful!

You are Resourceful, Radiant

and Responsible

S

Successful and Sophisticated

You are Successful and Sophisticated!

You are Supported, Sufficient and Skilled

T
Thankful

I am Thankful for you!

You are Teachable, Tenacious,

and Talented

U
Unique

You are Unique!

You are unbelievably unwavering and upbeat.

V

Vital

You are Vital to the world!

You are Versatile, Victorious

and a Visionary.

W
Winner

You are a Winner

You are Wonderful, Wise, and

Worthy.

X
Extraordinary

You are **Ex**traordinary!

You are Xenial and e**x**tremely exciting

Y

Youthful

You are Youthful!

You are Young-at-heart.

Z
Zeal

Your Zeal is amazing!

You have a very Zany

personality

Aa Bb Cc Dd Ee
Ff Gg Hh Ii Jj Kk
Ll Mm Nn Oo Pp
Qq Rr Ss Tt Uu
Vv Ww Xx Yy Zz

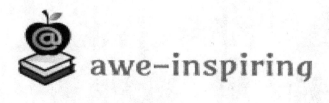 awe-inspiring

Printed in the USA
CPSIA information can be obtained
at www.ICGtesting.com
LVHW051557051224
798429LV00009B/234